OUR WORLD 4

SECOND EDITION • GRAMMAR WORKBOOK

Series Editors
Joan Kang Shin
JoAnn (Jodi) Crandall

T0302844

NATIONAL GEOGRAPHIC
LEARNING

Australia · Brazil · Mexico · Singapore · United Kingdom · United States

Unit 1

Comparatives with *-er*

I'm	**older**	**than**	you (are).
You're	**older**		I am / me.
Keiko is She's	**taller / shorter**		Masa. he is / him.
My cat is	**cuter**		your cat.
Dogs are	**friendlier**		cats.

Add ***-er***: tall ⟶ tall**er** old ⟶ old**er** short ⟶ short**er**
But: cute ⟶ cute**r** friendly ⟶ friendl**ier**

1 Read and write. Complete the sentences.

1. Jon is ___taller___ (tall) than his sister.
2. My mom is ______________ (young) than my dad.
3. My dad is ______________ (strong) than I am.
4. My teacher is ______________ (smart) than his students.
5. Are dogs ______________ (friendly) than cats?

2 Read and write. Write the opposite to complete the sentences.

1. My mom is short. Your mom is much ___taller than___ my mom.
2. My grandmother is old. Jake's grandmother is ______________ my grandmother.
3. Your school is small. My school is ______________ your school.
4. My brother's hamster is big. My sister's hamster is ______________ his hamster.
5. My cat is not friendly at all. Your cat is much ______________ my cat.

3 **Look and write.** Complete the sentences to compare the people.

1. Grandpa is taller than Dad.
2. Carlos is ______________ Mom and Dad.
3. Mom is ______________ Grandma.
4. Carlos is ______________ Grandma.
5. Grandma is ______________ Grandpa.
6. Mom's hair is ______________ than Grandma's hair.

4 **Write.** Compare the people and things.

1. one of your parents / you

____

2. two family members

____

3. your best friend / you

____

4. your teacher / your mom

____

5. your favorite wild animal / your pet

____

Present progressive for future plans

<table>
<tr><th colspan="5">Question</th><th colspan="4">Answer</th></tr>
<tr><td rowspan="4">What</td><td>are</td><td>you</td><td rowspan="4">doing</td><td>tonight?</td><td>I'm</td><td rowspan="4">going</td><td rowspan="4">to the store.</td><td>I'm = I am</td></tr>
<tr><td>is</td><td>she</td><td>tomorrow?</td><td>She's</td><td>She's = She is</td></tr>
<tr><td rowspan="2">are</td><td rowspan="2">they</td><td>on Sunday?</td><td rowspan="2">They're</td><td rowspan="2">They're = They are</td></tr>
<tr><td>after school?</td></tr>
</table>

Use *be* + verb-*ing* to talk about a definite future plan: *Tomorrow, I'<u>m going</u> to the store.*

1 **Read and write.** Use the words from the box.

do go make ~~play~~ ride shop take

1. Nathan __is playing__ soccer with friends at 5:00.
2. Grandma ______________ a cake this afternoon.
3. Keira and Nadia ______________ with their mom on Saturday morning.
4. The children ______________ the dog to the park this weekend.
5. When ______________ Fiona ______________ to the dentist?

2 **Write.** Use the words to say when people are doing these things.

1. My cousin / visit / me / at 3:00

   My cousin is visiting me at 3:00.

2. I / play / tennis / on Saturday afternoon

   ____

3. The students / go / to the museum / on Friday

   ____

4. My brother / take / the bus / to school / next week

   ____

5. What / Maria / do / tomorrow

   ____

3 **Look and write.** Answer the questions.

Lydia

Saturday		Sunday	
9:00:	go to swimming class	11:00:	play tennis
11:00:	shop with Mom	5:00:	visit Grandma
3:00:	have picnic at the park		

Ivan

Saturday		Sunday	
10:00:	go to library	11:00:	play tennis
11:00:	go to guitar class	7:00:	watch movie
3:00:	play soccer at the park		

1. What is Lydia doing on Saturday at 9:00?

   She's going to her swimming class.

2. What are Lydia and Ivan doing on Sunday at 11:00?

   ____

3. Where are Lydia and Ivan going on Saturday afternoon?

   ____

4. Who is Lydia visiting on Sunday afternoon?

   ____

5. What is Ivan doing on Sunday evening?

   ____

4 **Write.** Answer the questions about your weekend.

What are you doing on Saturday morning?

____

What are you doing on Sunday?

____

Are you visiting family this weekend?

____

Unit 2

Have to

I / You / We / They	**don't**	**have to**	cook	tomorrow.
She / He		**has to**		
	doesn't	**have to**		

Question					**Answer**
What	do	they	**have to**	do?	They **have to** cook lunch.
	does	he			He **has to** wash the lettuce.

Use *have to* in the negative for all forms: *You don't <u>have to</u> cook.*
He doesn't <u>have to</u> cook.

1 **Read.** Circle the correct answer.

My cousin Juan wants to have a garden. First, he **has to / have to** ask his parents. Then, they **have to / doesn't have to** buy seeds at the store. Juan **don't have to / has to** choose the vegetables he wants to grow. Then, he **has to / have to** dig and plant the seeds. What else **does he have to / do he have to** do? Of course, he and his family **doesn't have to / have to** remember to water the garden. The vegetables **have to / has to** get water to grow! Juan **doesn't have to / does have to** pick all of the vegetables at once. He can pick them as soon as they're ready.

2 **Read and write.** The girl is growing a garden. Complete the sentences.

1. She ________________ weed the garden.
2. She ________________ buy vegetables at the store.
3. She ________________ water the plants.

3 **Look and write.** Complete the questions and answers.

1. 

What would she like ______ with breakfast?

She 'd like some coffee ______.

2. 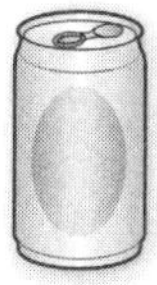

What ______ to drink?

They ______.

3. 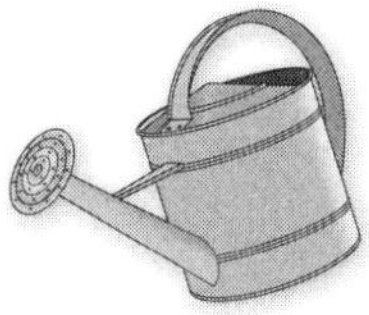

What ______ to do?

Grandma ______.

4. 

What ______ to play?

He ______.

4 **Read and write.** Answer the questions.

1. What would you like to have in your lunch box every day?

______

2. What would you like to have for dinner tonight?

______

3. What would you like to grow in a garden?

______

5 **Write.** You're ordering lunch at a restaurant. Write the dialogue.

WAITER: ______

YOU: ______

WAITER: ______

YOU: ______

Unit 3

Contrast with *but* and *instead*

Long ago, people used fire for light,	**but** today they use electric light.
Long ago, people used fire for light.	Today they use electric light **instead**.

Use a comma (,) before *but*.
Use *instead* at the end of the sentence.

1 **Read.** Complete the sentences with *but* or *instead.*

1. Many years ago, women wore long dresses, ________________ today many women wear shorter dresses and pants.
2. Long ago, many young children worked. Today they go to school ________________.
3. Long ago, families had many children, ________________ now families are smaller.
4. Many years ago, we grew our own food. Now we buy food from supermarkets ________________.

2 **Read and write.** Rewrite the sentences without the underlined word. Use *but* or *instead.*

1. Long ago, people made their own clothes, <u>but</u> today people buy them.
   Long ago, people made their own clothes. Today people buy them instead.
2. In 1900, people took boats to other countries. Now they take planes <u>instead</u>.
   ____
3. Many years ago, friends wrote letters on paper, <u>but</u> now friends send e-mails.
   ____
4. Long ago, children played outside every day. Now they play inside more <u>instead</u>.
   ____

3 **Look and write.** Finish the sentences using *but* or *instead.*

1.  Long ago, families told stories around a fire, but now they talk on cell phones.

2.  Many years ago, people used candles at night. ______________________

3. 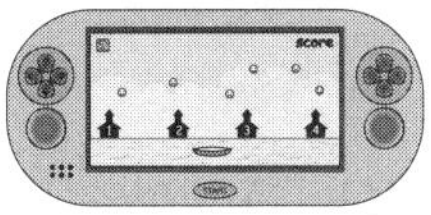 Many years ago, children played card games, ______________________

4 **Write.** Complete the sentences.

1. watch TV / read books

   When I was five, I watched TV every day. Now I read books instead.

2. walk / ride my bike

   When I was four, ______________________

3. write by hand / use computers

   Many years ago, people ______________________

5 **Write.** Complete the sentences. Use *but* or *instead.*

1. When I was younger, ______________________

2. Five years ago, ______________________

Comparatives with *more* + adjective

History is	more	interesting	than	math.
Cars are		expensive		bikes.
The new house is		modern		the old one.

Use *more* + adjective + *than* with . . .
- some two-syllable adjectives (*modern*)
- all adjectives with three or more syllables (*difficult, expensive, interesting*)

1 **Read.** Complete the sentences to compare the two things.

~~delicious~~ difficult modern old-fashioned

1. Food is more delicious today than it was 2,000 years ago.
2. Electric cars are ________________ than my parents' car.
3. My grandma's clothes are ________________ than my clothes.
4. Long ago, traveling was ________________ than it is today.

2 **Read and write.** Answer the questions.

1. What's more difficult–an English class or a science class?

   A science class is more difficult than an English class.
2. What's more delicious–cookies or ice cream?

   ____
3. What's more interesting–music or art?

   ____
4. What's more beautiful–the mountains or the ocean?

   ____

3 **Write.** Compare using a word from each column.

~~a computer~~	delicious	cold soup
electric light	exciting	chores
video games	~~expensive~~	candlelight
chocolate ice cream	important	board games
homework	modern	~~a pen and paper~~

1. A computer is more expensive than a pen and paper.
2. ______
3. ______
4. ______
5. ______

4 **Write.** Compare things you like. Use the words in the box.

beautiful delicious difficult expensive interesting modern

1. Two classes

______

2. Two movies

______

3. Two foods

______

4. Two animals

______

5. Two places

______

Review: Units 1–3

1 **Read.** Circle the letter.

1. What are you doing on Monday?
   a. I'm studying for a test.
   b. I have to study on Tuesday instead.
   c. I'd like to study on Mondays.
   d. I don't have to water the garden.
2. What would you like to eat?
   a. I have to eat vegetables every day.
   b. Meat is more expensive than vegetables.
   c. I'm eating eggplant from the garden.
   d. I'd like some green beans, please.
3. I'm not watering the garden this afternoon.
   a. I'm waiting for rain instead.
   b. I have to water the garden every afternoon.
   c. But my brother always waters the garden.
   d. I'm watering the garden instead.
4. Do you like eating onions?
   a. Yes, I'd like to eat cabbage.
   b. No, I don't, but I like cabbage.
   c. I do like cabbage, but I have to eat onions instead.
   d. Tomorrow I'm picking onions.

2 **Read.** Complete the sentences. Use *have to* or *-ing*.

1. I have a garden. I'm ______________ (plant) some vegetables in it.
2. I have some seeds. I ______________ (buy) them at the store.
3. Today I'm ______________ (dig) in the soil.
4. I ______________ (put) the seeds in and cover them with soil.
5. Then I ______________ (water) the seeds.
6. I'm ______________ (wait) for the vegetables to grow.
7. When the vegetables are ready, I ______________ (pick) them.

3 **Read.** Change the word in parentheses to compare.

When I was ______________ (young) than I am today, I had ______________ (curly) hair. I went to school, but I left school at age 15. I started to work, which was ______________ (interesting) to me. I didn't have a bike. I walked to work instead. The town was much ______________ (small) then. Today it's ______________ (difficult) to walk across town. Now it's ______________ (modern), with lots of tall, new buildings.

4 **Read and write.** Answer Marc's e-mail.

To: Dora Smith <smithd@email.com>
From: Marc Jones <marcjones@email.com>
Subject: Today

Hi Dora,

What are you doing today?
What chores do you have to do?
Would you like to go to the movies?
Or, would you like to play tennis instead?

Let me know!
Marc

To: Marc Jones <marcjones@email.com>
From: Dora Smith <smithd@email.com>
Re: Today

Hi Marc,

This morning I ______________________.
I ______________________.
I ______________________.
Let's meet at the bus stop at 2:00.

See you then,
Dora

5 **Write.** Write an e-mail to ask your friend about what he/she is doing, has to do, and would like to do this weekend. Use the e-mail from Activity 4 as a model.

____

____

____

____

Unit 4

Advice with *should*

I / You / He / She	**should**	study	for the test.	*shouldn't* = *should not*
	shouldn't	stay	inside all day.	

	Question					Answer
Ling is sick.	What	**should**	she	do?		She **should** stay in bed. She **shouldn't** go to school.
		Should	she	stay	home?	Yes, she **should**. No, she **shouldn't**.

Use *should* or *shouldn't* to ask for and give advice.

1 **Read.** Circle the correct answer.

1. Tom's sneezing a lot. He **should** / **shouldn't** use a tissue.
2. I have a fever. Do you think I **should** / **shouldn't** go to bed?
3. The children are all tired. They **should** / **shouldn't** go out to play.
4. Where **should** / **shouldn't** we put our first-aid kit?

2 **Read.** Write one answer with *should* and one with *shouldn't*.

1. All of the students have muddy hands.
   a. They ________________ wash their hands.
   b. They ________________ eat their snacks with muddy hands.
2. Hannah visits the dentist a lot.
   a. She ________________ eat candy.
   b. She ________________ brush her teeth two times a day.
3. My brother eats a lot of junk food.
   a. He ________________ do more exercise.
   b. He ________________ sit on the sofa all day.

3 **Write.** Unscramble the sentences. Give good advice.

1. should(n't) / fell / Julia / get / the first-aid kit / because / she

   ____

2. should(n't) / to / bed / go / Marco / because / has / a fever / he

   ____

3. should(n't) / you / have / cake / if / eat / a stomachache / you

   ____

4 **Look.** Write questions and answers.

1. 

   Me

   What should I do?

   You should get a first-aid kit.

2. 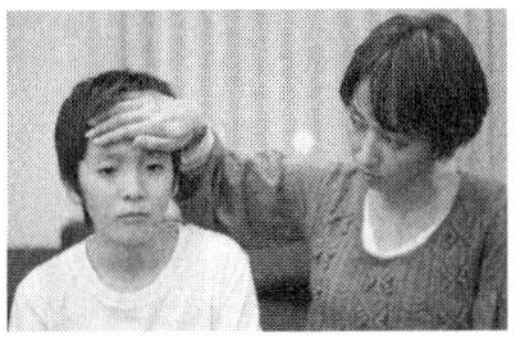

   Lee

   ____

   ____

3. 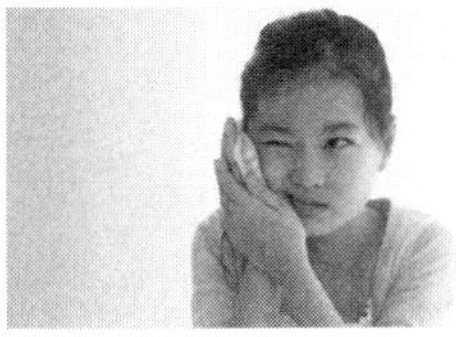

   My sister

   ____

   ____

4. 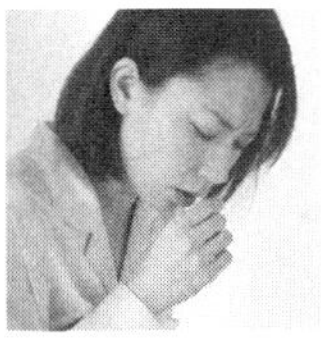

   My mom

   ____

   ____

5 **Write.** How can you take care of yourself? Write three things. Use *should* and *shouldn't*.

____

____

Reflexive pronouns

I	hurt	**myself**	while lifting the table.
You		**yourself**	
She		**herself**	
He		**himself**	
We		**ourselves**	
They		**themselves**	
The dog	hurt	**itself**	while running.

Compare: *I hurt **myself**.* = I hurt my own body.
*I made the first-aid kit **by myself**.* = I made the kit alone. No one helped me.

1 **Read.** Circle the letter.

1. I scratched ______.
   a. myself b. yourself c. himself
2. Did you burn ______?
   a. ourselves b. themselves c. yourself
3. We live by ______.
   a. yourselves b. ourselves c. themselves
4. The cat can take care of ______.
   a. yourself b. itself c. myself

2 **Read and write.** Use words from the box.

herself   myself   themselves   yourself

1. Can you help me put this bandage on?
   I'm busy right now. Can you please do it ________________?
2. Look how fast they can pedal on their bikes!
   They should be careful! They'll hurt ________________.
3. She doesn't have a costume to wear for the party.
   She can make one ________________.

3 **Read and write.** Make any necessary changes.

burn	cut	dry	hurt	~~take care of~~

1. Don't worry about Toby and me. We can take care of ourselves.
2. Timmy ______________ when he made the campfire.
3. Elsa fell off her bike, but she didn't ______________.
4. The children got out of the pool and ______________ with a towel.
5. I ______________ with scissors. I should be more careful!

4 **Read and write.**

1. Did their mom make dinner? No, they made dinner themselves.
2. Does your dad make your bed? No, I ______________
3. Did your grandmother make the cake? No, we ______________
4. Do you clean your cat? No, it ______________

5 **Write.** What things can you do by yourself? What do you like doing by yourself? Write four sentences.

I can get dressed by myself. I like reading by myself.

____

____

____

____

____

Unit 5

Superlatives with -*est* and *most*

I'm	the	**shortest**	student	in my class.
He's		**funniest**	actor	on TV.
She's		**smartest**	person	I know.
It's	the	**most** popular	food	on the menu.
They're		**most** famous	soccer players	in the world.

One syllable: *short* → ***the*** *short**est***   *smart* → ***the*** *smart**est***
Two syllables ending in *y*: *funny* → ***the*** *funn**iest***
Two or more syllables: *popular* → ***the most*** *popular*   *famous* → ***the most*** *famous*

1 **Write.** Organize the words. Change the forms.

amazing   brave   ~~cool~~   cute   ~~famous~~
funny   interesting   pretty   talented   wonderful

-est / -iest	*the most . . .*
the coolest	the most famous

2 **Read and write.** Complete the sentences.

1. I think snakes are the most interesting (interesting) animals of all.
2. My grandparents think Switzerland is ________________ (pretty) country.
3. This big history book is ________________ (boring) book in the library.

3 **Read.** Complete the sentences.

1. The Queen of England is a famous person.

   She's one of the most famous people __________ in the world.

2. Lionel Messi is a talented soccer player.

   He's ____________________ I know.

3. *Star Wars* is an amazing movie.

   I think it's ____________________ of all.

4. Venice is an interesting city.

   It's ____________________ to visit in the world.

5. A hamster is a cute pet.

   My brother says it's ____________________ of all.

4 **Write.** Give your opinion.

1. cute / animals Kittens are the cutest animals I know.
2. strong / superhero ____________________
3. beautiful / place ____________________
4. funny / family member ____________________
5. interesting / class ____________________
6. great / book ____________________

Irregular comparatives and superlatives

My cooking is	**good.**	**bad.**	
Volleyball is	**better**	**worse**	**than** basketball.
Green peppers are	**the best**	**the worst**	pizza topping.

The words *good* and *bad* have different comparative and superlative forms.

1 **Read.** Circle the correct word.

I think my dog Rover is the **best** / **better** dog in the world! He's my **worst** / **best** friend. He's smarter than other dogs. He's also **worse** / **good** at swimming. Rover can swim across the river, no problem! He loves playing ball. He's **better** / **the worst** at catching than I am. He's faster, too.

But sometimes Rover can be **the best** / **bad**. He loves eating my shoes! This is not a **good** / **better** thing. Now my shoes look **the worse** / **the worst** of all the students in my class. Rover may do **bad** / **worst** things, but I still think that he's the **better** / **best** pet!

2 **Read.** Complete the sentences.

1. Tanya is ___the worst___ friend of all. I fell off my bike, and she didn't even help me!
2. Today I'm really sick. I feel ________________ than I did yesterday.
3. I'm ________________ at playing video games than my dad. He's not very good.
4. Baseball is ________________ sport in the world. It's so fun!
5. ________________ thing about onions is that they make you cry.

3 **Look at one student's opinions.** Then write comparisons.

	☺	😐	☹
sports	soccer	basketball	baseball
food	chocolate ice cream	tomato soup	onions
pets	dog	hamster	goldfish

1. sports

   Soccer is the best sport! It's better than basketball. Baseball is the worst! It's so boring.

2. food

   ____

   ____

3. pets

   ____

   ____

4 **Write.** Now complete the table with your opinions. Then write sentences.

	☺	😐	☹
sports			
food			
pets			

____

____

____

Unit 6

Have to, must, can't, and don't

We	**must**	come	to school on time.
	have to		

You	**can't (must not)**	throw	trash in the street.	*can't = can not*
	Don't	throw	trash in the street.	*don't = do not*

To talk about rules, use *must, have to, can't,* and *don't.*

1 **Look and read.** Circle the correct answer.

1.  Everyone **has to** / **can't** pick up their trash.

2.  We **must** / **can't** recycle our bottles.

3.  People **have to** / **must not** fish in the river.

4.  You **must** / **can't** use your phone in the movie theater.

2 **Read and draw.**

1. You must not touch the sea turtles.

2. We have to recycle our trash.

3. Don't pollute the ocean!

3 **Read and write.** Use words from the box.

can't	don't	has to	have to	must	must not

1. **We're at the beach.**

   We have to protect the sea creatures. ___________ throw trash. ___________ wear a bathing suit.

2. **He's at a restaurant.**

   ___________ throw food. ___________ choose his lunch. ___________ bring his cat.

3. **They're at the zoo.**

   ___________ see the dolphins. ___________ miss the octopus. ___________ touch the shark.

4. **You're at home.**

   ___________ get up early for school. ___________ go to bed after eleven o'clock. ___________ make breakfast by myself.

4 **Read and write.** Answer the questions.

1. What must you do every day?

   ____

2. What do you have to do tomorrow?

   ____

3. What must you <u>not</u> do in school?

   ____

4. What can't you do before breakfast?

   ____

Future with *will* and *won't*

In the future,	we	**will**	know	more about the ocean floor.	*won't* = *will not*
	people	**won't**	drive	cars anymore.	

Question					**Answer**	
Where	**will**	we	live	in the future?	We**'ll** live in crowded cities. We **won't** live in small towns.	*we'll* = *we will*
	Will	people	live	longer?	Yes, they **will**. No, they **won't**.	

When you aren't 100% sure, use *maybe*.
In the future, will people live longer? / Maybe.

1 **Read.** Circle the letter of the sentence that describes the future.

1. a. We are overfishing, and it's hurting the ocean.
   b. I won't pollute the ocean.
2. a. An oil spill will affect the animals in the ocean.
   b. Pollution affects sea creatures.
3. a. Will the children pick up the trash on the beach?
   b. Do you always recycle your plastic trash?
4. a. I want to live under the sea.
   b. People won't live under the sea.

2 **Unscramble.** Look at pp. 94–95 of your Student's Book.

1. top / will / near / the / of / the / dolphins / swim / ocean
   Dolphins will swim near the top of the ocean.
2. oil spills / sea / harm / will / life
   ____
3. ocean's / creatures / middle layer / the / most / live / won't / in
   ____
4. sunlight / won't / bottom / the / of / the / ocean / reach
   ____

3 Read and write.

1. Robots ___will help___ (help) us with our work.
2. Tankers ________________ (not transport) oil across the ocean.
3. There ________________ (not be) trash in the sea in 100 years.
4. We ________________ (not use) plastic bottles or plastic bags.
5. People ________________ (take care of) the oceans better than they do now.

4 **Look at the Green Team's plan.** Answer the questions.

The Green Team will . . .

- ✓ clean up river banks.
- ✓ make "Keep It Clean" posters.
- ✓ invite people who live nearby to help.
- ✓ take bicycles not cars.
- ✓ camp in the park near the river.

1. What will the Green Team do next? ___They will clean up the river banks.___
2. Will they clean the beaches? ________________
3. What will they write on their posters? ________________
4. Who will help them? ________________
5. Will they travel in cars? ________________
6. Where will they camp? ________________

5 **Write.** What are four things you'll do to protect the planet? Use *will* and *won't*.

____

____

____

____

Review: Units 4–6

1 **Read.** Circle the correct answer.

Serena Williams is one of **more famous / the most famous** tennis players in the world. Williams is **more talented / most talented** than many other tennis players. She has won a lot of competitions, including gold medals at the Olympic Games. As a professional athlete, Williams **must / must not** take care of herself. Of course, she also **has to / must not** practice often.

Serena's sister, Venus Williams, is also a **popular / most popular** and talented tennis player. Sometimes the sisters play together on a team, and sometimes they play against each other. They are both **amazing / more amazing**!

2 **Read.** Circle the letter.

1. Is Rafa Nadal a good tennis player?
   - a. He's one of the tennis players.
   - b. He shouldn't play tennis.
   - c. He's one of the best tennis players in the world.
   - d. He's a better tennis player.
2. Did your mom make this cake? It's delicious.
   - a. No, she made it herself.
   - b. Yes, I made it myself.
   - c. No, she didn't. I made it myself.
   - d. Yes, by itself.
3. I feel sick. What should I do?
   - a. You should stay home.
   - b. Don't feel sick.
   - c. You shouldn't feel sick.
   - d. You won't feel sick.
4. What will happen to our oceans?
   - a. Our oceans shouldn't be polluted.
   - b. They will become more polluted.
   - c. We should continue overfishing.
   - d. We have to stop oil spills.

3 **Read and write.** Use words from the box.

can't	must	must not	will	won't

1. Don't eat too much candy or you ______________ get a toothache.
2. If you have a bad cut, you ______________ put a bandage on.
3. You should eat lots of fruit and vegetables so you ______________ get a cold.
4. If it's a very hot day, you ______________ forget to bring water with you.
5. I ______________ go to the party if I am sick.

4 **Look and write.** Compare the three items. Use the words in the box or any others you choose.

amazing	better/best	dangerous	delicious
friendly	popular	sweet	worse/worst

1.  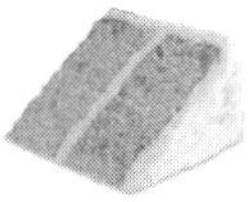 

____

____

2.   

____

____

5 **Write.** Write about an activity that you do. Compare it to another activity. Then give advice about it. Use the words in the box.

best/better	most	myself	should(n't)	will/won't

____

____

____

Unit 7

Used to for past habits

I	**used to**	play	outside.	These days	I play video games inside.
She					she plays video games inside.
Children					they play video games inside.
My friend	**didn't use to**	have	a computer.	Now	he has one.

Question						**Answer**
Where	did	you	**use to**	play?		I **used to** play in the park.
	Did	you	**use to**	play	in the park?	Yes, I did. / No, I didn't.

Used to is different from *be* + *used to.*
I used to do homework at night = I did this regularly in the past, but not anymore.
I am used to doing homework at night = I do this regularly. It is not a problem for me.

1 **Read.** Circle the correct answer.

1. How did children **used to** / **use to** play?
2. People didn't **used to** / **use to** have computers.
3. People **used to** / **use to** watch TV in black and white.
4. Did your grandparents **used to** / **use to** have a black and white TV?

2 **Read and write.** Complete the conversations.

1. How ___did___ people ___use to wash___ (wash) their clothes?
   They ___didn't use to have___ (not have) washing machines.
   They ________ (wash) their clothes by hand.
2. How ________ people ________ (take) a bath?
   They ________ (not have) water in their houses.
3. ________ children ________ (learn) with computers at school?
   No, they ________ (not learn) with computers at school.

3 **Look and write.** Complete the sentences about Jamie.

	At six years old	Now
home	apartment	house
sport	soccer	basketball
favorite food	grapes	cookies
pet	hamster	dog
hobbies	color pictures	take photos

1. Jamie used to live in an apartment. He didn't use to live in a house.
2. He ________________ color pictures. He ________________ take photos.
3. He ________________ a hamster. He ________________ a dog.
4. He ________________ soccer. He ________________ basketball.
5. His favorite food ________________ grapes. His favorite food ________________ cookies.

4 **Write.** Complete the chart like Jamie's. What used to be different for you? Choose categories and write sentences.

	At six years old	Now

I used to have long hair. I didn't use to wear glasses.

____

____

____

____

You for general statements

Question					Answer
What	can	you	do	on this computer?	**You** can play games and do homework.
How	do		make	vegetable soup?	First, **you** wash the vegetables. Then **you** . . .

you = people (in general)

1 **Rewrite the sentences.** Use *you* instead of the underlined words.

1. <u>People</u> should recycle batteries.

   ____

2. <u>All of the workers</u> must wear protective clothes.

   ____

3. <u>Students</u> don't have to use scissors.

   ____

4. <u>Families</u> can't feed the animals at the zoo.

   ____

2 **Unscramble.** Circle the number for sentences that are *not* about people in general.

1. should / plastic / you / recycle

   ____

2. my / help / bike / fix / you / me / can?

   ____

3. drink / to / you / water / need

   ____

4. scooter / should / a / you / new / get

   ____

3 **Look and write.** What do you use each item for? Write a sentence with *you.*

1.  ______________________________

2.  ______________________________

3.  ______________________________

4.  ______________________________

4 **Draw an invention.** Answer the questions.

1. What is it? ______________________
2. When do you use it? ______________________
3. How do you use it? ______________________
4. Why do you use it? ______________________

5 **Write.** Choose an object from the box. Explain how, when, and why you use it.

battery	bicycle	computer	first-aid kit	scissors	stove

____

____

Unit 8

Describing people with *who*

I have <u>a classmate</u>.	<u>She</u> likes math.
I have a classmate **who** likes math.	
Mateo has <u>two friends</u>.	<u>They</u> play basketball.
Mateo has two friends **who** play basketball.	
<u>The girl</u> is smart.	<u>She</u> sits next to me.
The girl **who** sits next to me is smart.	
<u>The people</u> are Canadian.	<u>They</u> live next door.
The people **who** live next door are Canadian.	

You can use *who* in a sentence to give more information about people.

1 **Read.** Complete the sentences with *who* where it is necessary. If *who* isn't necessary, write *X*.

1. The children _____ play video games together like to compete.
2. The children _____ are competing in the contest.
3. The boy _____ knows how to play every video game well.
4. The boy _____ gave me this controller lives across the street.

2 **Read.** Rewrite as one sentence.

1. My brother is a good swimmer. He loves diving.

   My brother is a good swimmer who loves diving.
2. My mom is a baker. She makes delicious cakes.

   ____
3. Abigail is a fast runner. She competes in sports.

   ____
4. Bai is a creative person. He has a great imagination.

   ____

3 **Write.** Write a sentence about each student's interests.

1. Akira / play in a musical group

   Akira is the student who plays in a musical group.

2. Rafa / enjoy taking care of animals

   ____

3. Kalinda / take beautiful photos

   ____

4. Jed / play baseball

   ____

5. Pablo / be good at math

   ____

4 **Write.** Complete the sentences. Use *who*.

1. A teacher is a person who helps students learn.
2. A doctor is someone ______________________________
3. A basketball player is an athlete ______________________________
4. My parents are people ______________________________
5. My best friend is someone ______________________________
6. Do you know a person ______________________________

5 **Write.** Write about two people. Use *who* and a word in the box.

be	collect	enjoy	help	listen	play	work

My brother is a person who enjoys inventing things.

____

____

Direct and indirect objects

Sara	gave	**me**	the pencil.			Object pronouns: me, you, her, him, us, them
Sara	gave		the pencil	**to**	**me**.	
My brother	made	**us**	breakfast.			
My brother	made		breakfast	**for**	**us**.	

The two sentences mean the same thing.

*Sara gave me the pencil. = Sara gave the pencil **to** me.*

With *make* and *buy*, use *for*: *Our teacher made / bought breakfast **for** us.*

1 **Read.** Match the sentences with the same meaning. Draw a line.

1. I showed my games to Nadia.
2. Nadia gave her games to me.
3. I sent two games to Beto and Nadia.
4. Beto sold some games to Nadia.
5. Beto sent some games to me and Nadia.
6. Nadia bought some games for Beto.

a. She bought him some games.
b. I sent them two games.
c. He sold her some games.
d. She gave me her games.
e. He sent us some games.
f. I showed her my games.

2 **Read.** Replace the underlined word(s).

her
1. My friends bought a dinosaur for Monica.
2. She showed the photo to her friends.
3. I sent an e-mail to my brother.
4. We found some old comic books for Ana and Ivan.
5. The children made a cake for me and Katherine.
6. I played a video game with my sister.

3 **Rewrite the sentences.** Use *her, them,* and *us.*

1. Lea made Grandma a birthday card.

    ____

2. Uncle Jon bought Clara and me some presents.

    ____

3. Bela gave the scientists the fossils she found.

    ____

4 **Write.** Rewrite each sentence from Activity 3. Use *to* or *for.*

1. ______________________________
2. ______________________________
3. ______________________________

5 **Read and write.** Answer the questions.

1. What did your friend give you for your birthday?

    My friend gave me a book for my birthday.

2. What clothing did your mom buy for you before school started?

    ____

3. What object did a teacher show students in your class this week?

    ____

4. What did you make for someone in your family?

    ____

5. Who did you send an important e-mail to this month?

    ____

Unit 9

Cause and effect with double comparatives

The more	she reads,	**the more**	she learns.
The more	I think about the problem,	**the more**	I worry about it.
The more	you push the swing,	**the higher**	it goes.
The more	we practice English,	**the better**	we will speak.

In each sentence, the first action causes the second action.

__The more__ she reads, __the more__ she learns.

first action second action

You can also use *will* with the second action.

The more she reads, the more she will learn.

1 **Read and match.** Draw a line.

1. The faster you pedal,
2. The harder I push my foot down,
3. The earlier you get up,
4. The more time they spend in the park,
5. The less I eat,

a. the more you can do in the morning.
b. the faster you'll get to school.
c. the hungrier I am.
d. the more fun they will have.
e. the faster my scooter goes.

2 **Read.** Check T for *True* and F for *False*. Then correct the false answers.

1. The ~~slower~~ faster she spins, the more difficult it is to stop. T F ✓
2. The less sugar you eat, the worse your teeth will be. T F
3. The earlier you go to bed, the less tired you will feel. T F
4. The less he pushes his friend, the higher he will go. T F
5. The more we stretch our muscles, the worse we will run. T F
6. The more force you use, the higher the ball goes. T F

3 **Read and write.** Complete the sentences with a word from the box.

better	cleaner	faster	harder	~~higher~~	worse

1. The stronger the wind, the ___higher___ the kite will go.
2. The less you practice, the ________________ it is to win.
3. The dizzier she gets, the ________________ she feels.
4. The more he pedals, the ________________ he goes.
5. The less plastic we use, the ________________ our oceans will be.
6. The more fruit you eat, the ________________ you will feel.

4 **Read and write.** Complete the sentences.

1. The more water a flower gets, ____.
2. The less I talk, ____.
3. The more vegetables children eat, ____.
4. The longer my friends and I play outside, ____.

5 **Write.** Write about your own activities. Use the words in the box.

better	less
earlier	longer
faster	more
harder	sooner
later	worse

The more I watch TV, the less I study.

____

____

____

____

Definitions with *which*

Gravity is <u>a force</u>.	<u>It</u> pulls you toward Earth.
Gravity is a force **which** pulls you toward Earth.	
A carnivore is <u>an animal</u>.	<u>It</u> eats meat.
A carnivore is an animal **which** eats meat.	
Skates are special <u>shoes</u>.	You wear <u>them</u> on the ice.
Skates are special shoes **which** you wear on the ice.	
Honey is a sweet <u>food</u>.	Bees make <u>it</u>.
Honey is a sweet food **which** bees make.	

You can use *which* to combine sentences.

1 **Read.** Write *which* when necessary. If it's not necessary, write *X*.

1. Gravity ______________ pulls you toward the center of the earth.
2. Gravity is the force ______________ holds everything in place.
3. Tennis is a sport ______________ needs two or four people.
4. I play tennis ______________ with three of my school friends.
5. Pedaling ______________ makes a bicycle move.

2 **Write.** Use *which* and the words provided.

1. ice cream / sweet food / eat when it's hot outside.

   Ice cream is a sweet food which you eat when it's hot outside.

2. markers / tools / use to color pictures

   ____

3. basketball / sport / play with an orange ball

   ____

4. butterfly / insect / have beautiful wings

   ____

5. swing / object / move forward and backward

   ____

3 **Write.** Complete the sentences using *which*.

1. A computer is an invention which we use all the time.
2. ________ is an object ________.
3. ________ is a language ________.
4. ________ is a sport ________.
5. ________ is a game ________.
6. ________ is a fruit ________.

4 **Look and write.** Describe each object using *which*.

1. 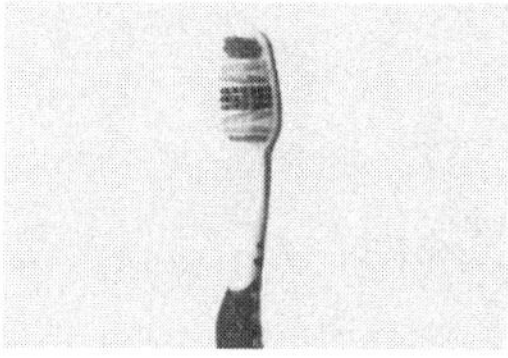

A toothbrush is something which you use to clean your teeth.

2. 

____

3. 

____

4. 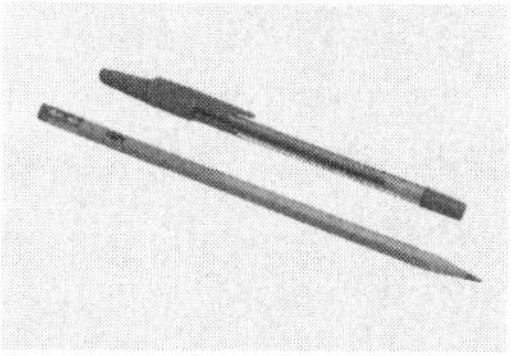

____

5 **Write.** Choose an object in your classroom. Write three clues to describe it. Use *which*.

____

Review: Units 7–9

1 **Read.** Circle the letter.

1. She is the teacher ______ told me to study more.

   a. which b. who c. to

2. The more she sings, the ______ she is.

   a. happier b. more c. less

3. They ______ be our neighbors.

   a. use to b. used c. used to

4. An e-mail is a message ______ you send from your computer.

   a. when b. which c. who

5. She bought a book ______ because she knows I love reading.

   a. for me b. to me c. me

6. I ______ to eat broccoli, but now I love it.

   a. used b. didn't used c. didn't use

7. You should send ______ a text.

   a. Mauricio b. to Mauricio c. for Mauricio

8. ______ add the numbers together to get the total.

   a. Your b. You c. Who

2 **Write.** Complete the sentences with *who* or *which*.

1. A *quill* is something ______________ people used to write with.
2. He's a boy ______________ has a lot of hobbies.
3. The friends ______________ are coming to lunch today are from Italy.
4. Friction is a force ______________ causes a moving object to slow down.

3 **Read.** Complete the story. Use words from the box.

didn't use to	for	less	them	used to	which	who	you

Nala and Talib ______________ walk two hours to school every day when they were children. Their parents were farmers ______________ lived in a small village. Their home was far from the school, so the earlier they got up, the ______________ they had to hurry. Their mother used to make food ______________ them to take on their long journey. Their father told ______________ every day to be careful. Each child had a backpack ______________ was filled with heavy books. They ______________ stop at all because they knew the rule: ______________ had to be in your seat before the teacher came into the classroom.

4 **Read.** Rewrite the sentences. Use the words in parentheses.

1. When I was younger, I played card games with my cousins. (*used to/use to*)

   ____

2. My brother made me a new avatar. (*for*)

   ____

3. In the past, people didn't play video games. (*used to/use to*)

   ____

4. He gave me a fossil from his collection. (*to*)

   ____

5 **Write.** Complete the sentences about yourself.

1. The harder I ____
2. The more my teacher ____
3. The better I ____

Review: Units 1–9

1 Read. Circle the correct answer to each question.

1. What would you like?
   a. I like strawberries.
   b. I'd like a chicken salad.
2. What does she have to do tomorrow?
   a. She has a beautiful garden.
   b. She has to water the garden.
3. I have a scratch. What should I do?
   a. You should wash it with soap and water.
   b. We must scratch ourselves.
4. Did she send the letter to her brother?
   a. Yes, she sent him the letter.
   b. No, he didn't send her the letter.
5. What did people use to do in their spare time?
   a. They used games.
   b. They used to play games.
6. What are they doing this weekend?
   a. They're watching the baseball game.
   b. They usually watch baseball.
7. Will we have computers in our bodies in the future?
   a. No, we don't.
   b. No, we won't.
8. What do you need to be an inventor?
   a. You need creativity and imagination.
   b. You are a creative person.

2 Read. Circle the correct answer.

1. Do they **should** / **have to** compete to win the game?
2. The winner **don't** / **must** get the highest score.
3. I **like** / **would like** to learn more about this invention.
4. I **have to** / **can't** read my comic books when I have homework.
5. We **should** / **must not** touch the paintings in the museum.
6. You **must** / **shouldn't** go on roller coasters if you feel dizzy.

3 **Read and write.** Use the words in parentheses.

1. Sea sponges are much ________________ (amazing) than my plants.
2. Coral reefs are ________________ (beautiful) places in the ocean.
3. The pollution in our oceans is ________________ (bad) than ever before.
4. The more you swim, ________________ (strong) you will be.
5. The more I read about the ocean, ________________ (good) I understand it.

4 **Read.** Complete the paragraph. Use words from the box.

didn't use to	herself	instead	is selling	the more
myself	used to	which	who	will

My aunt is a person ________________ loves to help others. Tomorrow she ________________ her delicious bread to neighbors and friends. The more bread she sells, ________________ money she will make. She ________________ give this money to a local school. My aunt ________________ sell her bread to everybody. She ________________ have an electric stove. ________________, she had a very big wood-burning stove ________________ needed a lot of wood to burn. My aunt burned ________________ so often in those days. I'm helping her make the bread for tomorrow—I hope I don't burn ________________!

5 **Read and write.** Change the underlined parts of each sentence. Don't change the meaning.

1. My little sister <u>got a cut on her body</u>.

____

2. I used to collect seashells, <u>but</u> now I like to go swimming.

____

3. We <u>are going to</u> work on our invention to make it better.

____

4. The students told <u>their teacher</u> their ideas.

____

6 **Look and write.** Complete the sentences. Use *who* or *which*.

1.  Marco is a boy ________________________________.

2.  She is using a machine ________________________________.

3.  Checkers is a game ________________________________.

7 **Write.** Choose a family member. Answer the questions.

1. What are you doing the next time you see this person?

____

2. What did this person use to do in the past?

____

3. Compare this person to yourself. Write two sentences.

____

8 **Write.** Write a paragraph about yourself. Describe your past, your present, and your future. Use the words in the box.

good	have to	instead	the (more)	must
myself	should	used to	who	will

____

____

____

____

GAME

Read the clues. Write the words in the correct squares. Then write the secret message below.

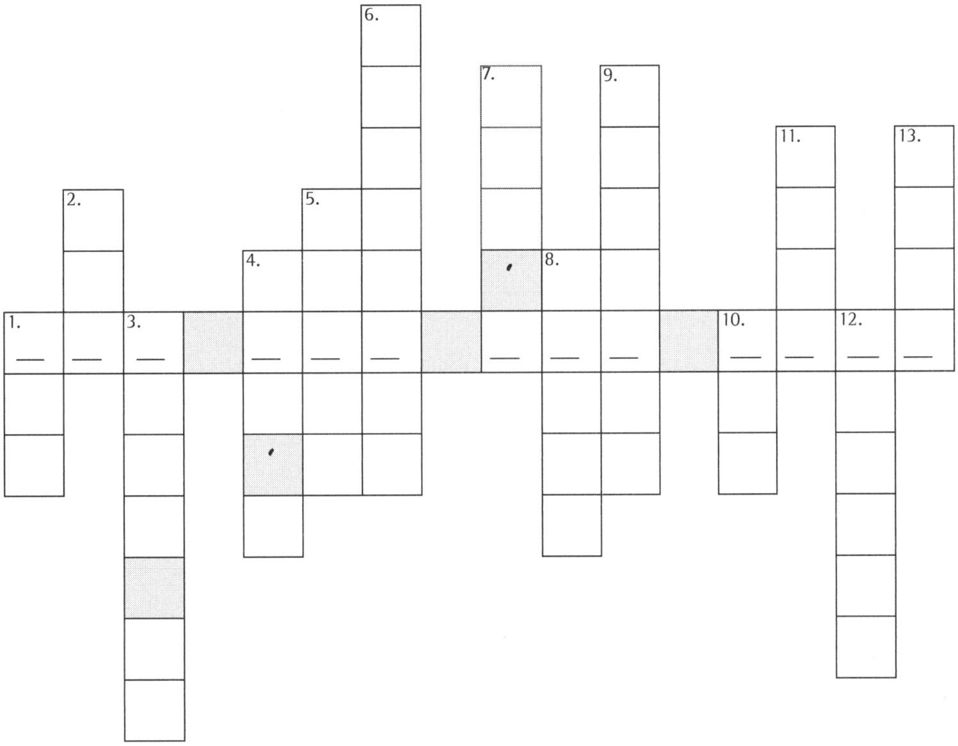

1. __________ need an imagination to invent things.
2. The boy __________ broke his leg is wearing a cast.
3. I __________ love teddy bears when I was younger.
4. You __________ throw your trash into the ocean.
5. An oil spill is one of the __________ things that can happen to our oceans.
6. Can you make the cake __________, or would you like me to help you?
7. In my opinion, people __________ be able to explore all the world's oceans. They're too big!
8. An octopus is an animal __________ has eight legs.
9. Gina doesn't collect fossils. She collects seashells __________.
10. I don't have a fever, __________ I do have a bad cold.
11. The __________ you pedal, the faster you go.
12. He is very creative. We __________ buy him a camera for his birthday.
13. We __________ protect our oceans and the animals that live there.

The secret message is: _ _ _ _ _ _ _ _ _ _ _ _ _ !